Farmyard Security

A Readers' Theater
Script and Guide

By Nancy K. Wallace • Illustrated by Michelle Henninger

magic
wagon

To my daughters, Mollie and Elizabeth, who have spent endless hours helping with library plays! —NKW

Published by Magic Wagon, a division of the ABDO Group, PO Box 398166, Minneapolis, Minnesota 55439. Copyright © 2014 by Abdo Consulting Group, Inc. International copyrights reserved in all countries. All rights reserved. No part of this book may be reproduced in any form without written permission from the publisher.

Looking Glass Library™ is a trademark and logo of Magic Wagon.

Printed in the United States of America, North Mankato, Minnesota.
042013
092013
♻ This book contains at least 10% recycled materials.

Written by Nancy K. Wallace
Illustrations by Michelle Henninger
Edited by Stephanie Hedlund and Rochelle Baltzer
Cover and interior design by Renée LaViolette

Library of Congress Cataloging-in-Publication Data
Wallace, Nancy K.
  Farmyard security : a readers' theater script and guide / written by Nancy K. Wallace ; illustrated by Michelle Henninger.
     pages cm. -- (Readers' theater: how to put on a production)
  ISBN 978-1-61641-985-1
1. Chickens--Juvenile drama. 2. Fairy tales--Adaptations--Juvenile drama. 3. Theater--Production and direction--Juvenile literature. 4. Readers' theater--Juvenile literature. I. Henninger, Michelle, illustrator. II. Title.
  PS3623.A4436F38 2013
  812'.6--dc23

3 1561 00256 0765

2013006050

Table of Contents

School Plays

Do you like to act, create props, make weird sound effects, or paint scenery? You should put on a production. Plays are lots of fun! And a play is a great way for kids to work together as a team.

Readers' theater can be done very simply. You just read your lines. You don't have to memorize them! Adapted readers' theater is more like a regular play. The performers wear makeup and costumes. The stage has scenery and props. The cast moves around to show the action. But, performers can still read their scripts.

Does your class want to donate money to a food shelf? Does your school need money to buy new computers? Plays can also be fund-raisers. You can sell tickets to your production and raise money for a good cause!

You will need a space large enough to put on your production. An auditorium with a stage is ideal. A classroom will work, too. Now, choose a date and get permission to use the space.

Finally, make flyers or posters to advertise your play. Place them around your school and community. Tell your friends and family. Everyone enjoys watching kids perform!

Cast & Crew

There are many people needed to put on a production. First, decide who will play each part. Each person in the cast will need a script. All the performers should practice their lines.

Farmyard Security needs the following cast:

Narrator - The storyteller

Henrietta Hen - A scatterbrained chicken

Rusty Rooster - Pretends that he is brave but he really isn't

Panicky Pig - Worries a lot about having enough food

Calamity Cow - Chews gum and dawdles behind the rest

Paranoid Puppy - Wants to be in charge but is just as scared as the rest of the animals

Wily Wolf - Tries to lure the animals into his cave

Farmer Jones - Is very reasonable and practical

Next, a crew is needed. The show can't go on without these important people! Some jobs can be combined for a small show. Every show needs a director. This person organizes everything and everyone in the show.

The director will work with the production crew. This includes the costume designers. Stage managers make sure things run smoothly.

Your production can also have a stage crew. This includes lighting designers to run spotlights and other lighting. Set designers plan and make scenery. The special effects crew takes care of sound and other unusual effects.

Sets & Props

At a readers' theater production, the performers sit on stools at the front of the room. But, an adapted readers' theater production or a full play requires some sets and props.

Sets include a background for each scene of the play. Props are things you'll need during the play. You'll also need tickets that list the title of the play and where it will take place. List the date and time of your performance.

Your production can also have a playbill. It is a printed program. The front of a playbill has the title, date, and time of the play. Playbills list all of the cast and production team inside.

Farmyard Security could have the following set and props:

Scene Sets - The farm with a barn made of cardboard at center stage, an apple tree at stage left, Farmer Jones's house, and a forest of cardboard trees.

Props - A hay bale, several real or plastic apples that can be dropped on the stage, a tractor made of cardboard or a wagon decorated as a tractor, and finally a wagon to pull behind the tractor.

Makeup & Costumes

The stage and props aren't the only things people will be looking at in your play! The makeup artist has a big job. Stage makeup needs to be brighter than regular makeup. Even boys wear stage makeup!

Costume designers set the scene just as much as set designers. They will borrow costumes or adapt old clothing for each character. The costumes for *Farmyard Security* can all be made out of different colored sweatshirts. Ask adults if you need help finding or sewing costumes.

Farmyard Security performers will need these costumes:

Narrator - A flannel shirt and jeans

Henrietta Hen - Brown sweats with a yellow felt beak and a red comb for the top of her head, add cardboard or felt wings

Rusty Rooster - Red sweats with a yellow felt beak and a much larger comb than Henrietta's comb, add wings and a felt tail

Panicky Pig - Pink sweats with pink felt pig ears attached to a headband, a paper cup can be tied on as a snout, use a large pink pipe cleaner to make a curly tail

Calamity Cow - Black pants and a white sweatshirt painted with black spots, make a braided tail out of yarn

Paranoid Puppy - Gray or black sweats, sew floppy, felt dog ears to a
　　headband, make a tail out of felt

Wily Wolf - Brown sweats with a felt tail sewed on them, felt wolf ears
　　attached to a headband

Farmer Jones – A flannel shirt, jeans, and a straw hat

Stage Directions

When your sets, props, and costumes are ready, it is important to rehearse. Choose a time that everyone can attend. Try to have at least five or six rehearsals before your show. You should practice together as a team even if you will be reading your scripts for readers' theater.

A play should sound like a conversation. Try to avoid pauses when no one is speaking. You can do this by adding sound effects. The sound designer for *Farmyard Security* could break a stick in half to make a cracking sound when the branch breaks in Scene One. In Scene Two, knock loudly on something wooden back stage when Henrietta knocks on Farmer Jones's door.

Some theater terms may seem strange. The *wings* are the sides of the stage that the audience can't see. The *house* is where the audience sits. The *curtains* refers to the main curtain at the front of the stage.

When reading your script, the stage directions are in parentheses. They are given from the performer's point of view. You will be facing the audience when you are performing. Left will be on your left and right will be on your right. When rehearsing, perform the stage directions and the lines to get used to moving around the stage.

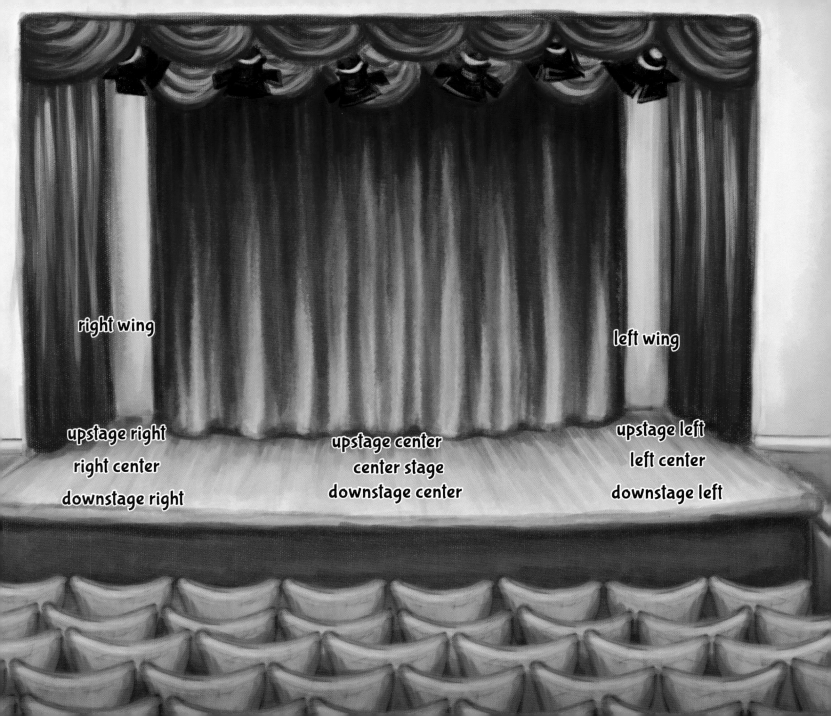

Script: *Farmyard Security*

(Opening of the Curtain: The barn should be at upstage center. An apple tree stands at stage left. The animals are arranged in a large circle. Rusty Rooster is lying on a hay bale. Panicky Pig is asleep by the tractor. Calamity Cow is sleeping by the wagon. The narrator sits on a stool at stage right removed from the action.)

Narrator: Once upon a time there was a cozy little farm at the edge of a big forest. Most days, the farm was peaceful and quiet. But one day, a very small chicken caused a great big problem. It was late one afternoon and most of the animals were napping. They were dreaming of food buckets full of delicious treats.

(Henrietta Hen enters from stage left and goes over to sit under the apple tree. She clucks quietly as she walks.)

Narrator: It was warm and sunny. Henrietta Hen decided to nestle under an apple tree in the orchard. She tucked her head under her wing. In just a few minutes, she was sound asleep.

(Henrietta Hen curls up with her head under one arm.)

Narrator: Right above her, the apple tree's branches were loaded with fruit. There were so many apples that all of a sudden, a branch cracked loudly. Several big, red apples fell off the tree. One apple hit Henrietta Hen in the head!

(Loud snapping sound from back stage. Drop three or four apples and let them roll across the stage. Henrietta jumps up and rubs her head.)

Henrietta: *Cluck! Cluck! Cluck!* Oh my goodness, the sky must be falling! I have to tell Farmer Jones right away!

Narrator: Henrietta Hen ran down the path toward the barn, squawking loudly. She found Rusty Rooster sleeping peacefully on a hay bale.

Henrietta: Oh, Rusty Rooster, wake up!

Rusty Rooster: *(Rubbing his eyes)* What is the matter with you? Can't you see I was taking my afternoon nap?

Henrietta: Rusty Rooster, the sky is falling! We have to run and tell Farmer Jones!

Rusty Rooster: *(Looking up)* What do you mean the sky is falling? Everything looks perfectly all right to me.

Henrietta: It's not all right! I was sound asleep in the orchard and I heard the sky crack. Then a piece of it fell and hit me on the head!

Rusty Rooster: *(Looking around nervously and flapping his wings)* Oh dear! Well, maybe we should tell Farmer Jones! I'll come along with you.

(Rusty Rooster and Henrietta Hen should lift their knees high as though they are running. They flap their wings and cluck loudly as they walk to Panicky Pig.)

17

Narrator: The two chickens ran down the road clucking and squawking. They ran to Panicky Pig, who was snoozing by the tractor.

Henrietta: Oh, Panicky Pig, wake up! Wake up! The sky is falling!

Panicky Pig: (Stretches and looks up) What do you mean the sky is falling?

Henrietta: I was sound asleep and I heard it crack. Then a big piece of it fell and hit me on the head!

Panicky Pig: Oh my goodness! That's terrible! What should we do?

Henrietta: We are going to tell Farmer Jones. Do you want to come with us?

Panicky Pig: (Looking up at the sky and acting frightened) Of course, I want to come with you! I'm afraid to be caught out here alone when

the sky falls down! Do you think we'll be back before dinner?

Henrietta: Don't worry about food! Just hurry!

Narrator: Now the silly chickens and Panicky Pig raced down the road making a lot of noise. Calamity Cow was napping beside the hay wagon.

(*Chickens cluck and Pig oinks. They pretend to run as they approach Calamity Cow.*)

Henrietta: Calamity Cow! You have to wake up! The sky is falling! Please come with us to tell Farmer Jones!

Calamity Cow: (*Yawns and looks up*) Don't be ridiculous! How can the sky be falling? It looks perfectly normal to me. It's actually a very pretty blue today with just a few fluffy, white clouds.

Henrietta: I just heard the sky crack! And a big piece of it fell and hit me on the head!

Calamity Cow: (*Looking worried and glancing at the sky*) Oh my, that does sound serious! Maybe I'd better come along, too. There's no sense in taking any chances.

(*Henrietta Hen, Rusty Rooster, Panicky Pig, and Calamity Cow exit stage right together.*)

Scene change: Stage crew remove the barn and place farmhouse at upstage center. Henrietta Hen, Rusty Rooster, Panicky Pig, and Calamity Cow all enter stage left.

Narrator: Now all the silly animals raced down the road until they reached Farmer Jones's house. They scrambled up on the porch. Henrietta Hen knocked at the door.

Henrietta: Hello? Hello? Farmer Jones?

(Pause quietly while everyone looks expectantly at the farmhouse.)

Paranoid Puppy: *(Enters stage right)* No one is home, Henrietta.

Henrietta: Oh *cluck, cluck, cluck*! What will we do now?

Paranoid Puppy: I'm the watchdog. Farmer Jones leaves me in charge of farmyard security while he is away. What's going on?

Henrietta: Oh! There's a terrible problem! We're doomed!

Paranoid Puppy: (*In a brave voice*) Well, you'll be safe here. I'll protect you! We'll wait here on the porch until Farmer Jones comes back.

Panicky Pig: The porch isn't safe! If the sky falls, the porch will be crushed and so will we!

Paranoid Puppy: Why would the sky fall down? We haven't had a problem with it in years!

Henrietta: Well, I heard it crack and a piece of it hit me on the head. We probably have very little time to save ourselves! Let's head for the woods! There is probably somewhere there that we can hide!

Rusty Rooster: I don't know, Henrietta. Going to the woods doesn't sound safe to me. There are lots of wild animals in the woods.

Henrietta: *(Hands on her hips)* Do you have a better idea?

Rusty Rooster: No, not really.

Henrietta: Well, I'm going to the woods! The rest of you can do whatever you like. *(Henrietta turns and walks off stage right.)*

Panicky Pig: Oh dear, I wish I'd brought a snack! Well, I'm not getting crushed! I'm with her. *(Walks off stage right.)*

Calamity Cow: Me, too! *(Follows Panicky Pig.)*

Rusty Rooster: *(Running after them)* I guess it's better to be safe than sorry.

Paranoid Puppy: (*Looking behind him at the house*) Wait for me! I'm coming, too!

Scene change: Stage crew remove the farmhouse and apple tree. Add several cardboard or fake trees to the stage for the woods.

Narrator: Now all those silly animals went down the road to the woods. They were making a lot of noise!

(*The animals enter from stage left. The chickens are clucking, the cow is mooing, the pig oinks, and the puppy barks.*)

Narrator: Wily Wolf lived on the hill. He heard them coming from a mile away. He slunk down and peered through the trees to see what was going on.

(*Wily Wolf appears from stage right and begins to slink around the trees. He pops up in front of the farmyard animals.*)

Wily Wolf: Good afternoon, friends!

Animals: OH NO!!!
(Sounding very afraid. All of them back up and fall into a big heap together except Henrietta Hen.)

Henrietta: *(Her voice quivering)* Hello, Wily Wolf!

Wily Wolf: Why, Henrietta Hen, what are you doing in my part of the woods?

Henrietta: The sky is falling! We wanted to tell Farmer Jones but we can't find him!

Narrator: Now, wolves are terribly clever. Wily Wolf saw a chance to feed his family for weeks!

Wily Wolf: *(In a sly voice)* Oh, Henrietta, did you say that the sky is falling? Why, that is terrible! Why don't you all come right up to my cave? You'll be safe there if the sky falls.

Rusty Rooster: *(Whispering)* Henrietta, that's a really bad idea!

Henrietta: *(Looking around nervously)* Well, I don't know what to do. We can't stay out here.

Wily Wolf: *(Throws his arms out in welcome)* Henrietta, please don't worry! My cave is the safest place to be if the sky really is falling. And my wife, Fiona, is an extreme couponer! She saves us hundreds of dollars in groceries every month. Our cave is stocked from the floor to the ceiling with food and supplies! You and your friends could live comfortably there with us for years and we would always have enough to eat!

Henrietta: Really?

Panicky Pig: *(Wiping forehead)* Well, that's a relief! We wouldn't want to run out of food, now would we?

Wily Wolf: My cave is so very warm and cozy. There is more than enough room for all!

Henrietta: I guess it would be all right, then. *(Pats Wily Wolf on the arm.)* How kind you are. Isn't Wily Wolf kind, Rusty Rooster?

Rusty Rooster: *(Nodding)* He certainly is.

Calamity Cow: Thank you so much, Wily Wolf! We were so lucky that we ran into you today! Can you show us the way to your cave?

Panicky Pig: I'm glad that's decided. I will be so happy to be somewhere safe. Besides, it's almost time for dinner.

Wily Wolf: (Laughing softly and motioning them forward) Come right this way, then. Let me welcome you to your new home!

(Animals should make soft noises as they walk in a circular motion around the stage following the wolf.)

Narrator: So Wily Wolf led all the silly animals up the road, through the woods, and to his cave. But just before they were about to go inside, Farmer Jones came walking down the road from the market.

(Farmer Jones enters stage left. Wily Wolf backs away with his hands up.)

Farmer Jones: Stop! Stop! Where are you going, Henrietta Hen?

Henrietta: The sky is falling! We tried to tell you but we couldn't find you! Wily Wolf offered to take us into his cave where we will be safe. Would you like to come with us?

Farmer Jones: What makes you think the sky is falling?

Henrietta: Well, I heard it crack and a big piece of it hit me on the head!

Farmer Jones: Henrietta, where were you when this piece of sky fell?

Henrietta: I was taking a lovely nap under the apple tree.

Farmer Jones: What did this piece of sky look like?

Henrietta: *(Puts a finger to her forehead as though she is thinking)* Well, let me see if I can remember. It all happened so fast! I think it was big, round, and red!

Farmer Jones: Could it have been an apple that hit you on the head?

Henrietta: Well, let me think. Apples are . . .

Rusty Rooster: *(Speaking slowly and distinctly)* Big and round and red!

Henrietta Hen: Oh! So I guess it could have been . . .

All animals together: An apple!

Panicky Pig: You silly chick! You led us right to the wolf's den!

Wily Wolf: (*Rubbing his hands together*) Yes, she did. So if you will just come inside now, I'll have my wife make dinner! Shall we start with roast chicken tonight?

Farmer Jones: Run!

(*Farmer Jones and animals exit stage left, clucking, oinking, mooing, and barking.*)

Narrator: And so Henrietta Hen, Rusty Rooster, Panicky Pig, Calamity Cow, Paranoid Puppy, and Farmer Jones ran down the hill to the farm as fast as they could! And poor Wily Wolf, well, he and his wife had to eat veggie burgers for dinner!

The End

Adapting Readers' Theater Scripts

Readers' theater can be done very simply. You just read your lines. You don't have to memorize them! Performers sit on chairs or stools. They read their parts without moving around.

Adapted Readers' Theater
This is more like a regular play. The performers wear makeup and costumes. The stage has scenery and props. The cast moves around to show the action. Performers can still read their scripts.

Hold a Puppet Show
Some schools and libraries have puppet collections. Students make the puppets be the actors. They read their scripts.

Teacher's Guides

Readers' Theater Teacher's Guides are available online. Each guide includes reading levels for each character and additional production tips for each play. Visit Teacher's Guides at **www.abdopublishing.com** to get yours today!